MW00781024

Air Fryer Cookbook for Beginners 2021

Simple, Easy, Low-Carb and Delish Recipes for Smart People on a Budget

Written By

Marion Bartolini

© Copyright 2021 - All rights reserved.

The content contained within this book may not be reproduced, duplicated or transmitted without direct written permission from the author or the publisher.

Under no circumstances will any blame or legal responsibility be held against the publisher, or author, for any damages, reparation, or monetary loss due to the information contained within this book. Either directly or indirectly.

Legal Notice:

This book is copyright protected. This book is only for personal use. You cannot amend, distribute, sell, use, quote or paraphrase any part, or the content within this book, without the consent of the author or publisher.

Disclaimer Notice:

Please note the information contained within this document is for educational and entertainment purposes only. All effort has been executed to present accurate, up to date, and reliable, complete information. No warranties of any kind are declared or implied. Readers acknowledge that the author is not engaging in the rendering of legal, financial, medical or professional advice. The content within this book has been derived from various sources. Please consult a licensed professional before attempting any techniques outlined in this book.

By reading this document, the reader agrees that under no circumstances is the author responsible for any losses, direct or indirect, which are incurred as a result of the use of information contained within this document, including, but not limited to, — errors, omissions, or inaccuracies.

Table of Contents

INTRODUCTION 9

BREAKFAST RECIPES 11

    Breakfast banana oatmeal...12

    Classic baked oatmeal 14

    Old-fashioned granola 16

    Mushroom and rice bake...18

    Dried berry bread pudding 20

BRUNCH RECIPES 23

    Sausage egg cups 24

LUNCH RECIPES...27

    Kipper and balmy orange gravy....................................28

    Kipper and pansies 29

    Kipper strips and pinecone mix 30

    Easy kipper strips and bell peppers 31

    Kipper and citrus dressing 32

    Redfish paella 33

    Kipper and capers..34

    Kipper and jasmine rice 35

    Kipper and carrots 36

    Black cod & plum sauce 37

    Fried branzino...39

    French style cod...40

    Cubed salmon chili..42

    Creamy tuna cakes 44

DINNER RECIPES 45

    Cheeseburger-stuffed bell peppers 46

Steak and veggie kebabs 48

Korean BBQ beef bowls 50

SIDE DISH RECIPES... 53

Batter-fried scallions 54

Heirloom tomato with baked feta 55

CASSEROLES 57

Creamy cheesy tomato casserole 58

CHICKEN AND POULTRY 59

Classic smoked pork chops 60

Pork ribs with red wine sauce 62

Pork with buttery broccoli 64

Pork sausage with mashed cauliflower............................... 66

BEEF, STEAK AND LAMB RECIPES 69

Rosemary beef chuck roast... 70

Beef round roast with carrots 72

FISH AND SEAFOODS... 75

Cod fillets and peas 76

Coconut coated fish cakes with mango sauce 77

Teriyaki glazed halibut steak... 79

FRUIT AND VEGETABLES 81

Platter of brussels and pine nuts 82

SNACK RECIPES.. 83

Banana fritters 84

Tasty banana snack 85

Strawberry cobbler 86

Super yummy brownies 88

Grilled scallion cheese sandwich 89

APPETIZER RECIPES 91

Maple carrot fries 92

PASTA AND RICE RECIPES 93

Spanish Rice 94

BREAD & GRAINS 95

Sunflower seeds bread 96

DESSERT RECIPES 99

Mixed berry crumble 100

Apple blueberry hand pies 101

Oatmeal carrot cookie cups...103

Dark chocolate oatmeal cookies 105

Tasty banana and cinnamon cake 107

Delicious banana bread 108

Easy to make air fried bananas..110

Dark Chocolate Truffles 111

Rum Cake...112

CONCLUSION 113

INTRODUCTION

Thank you for purchasing this book!

The air fryer has a heating ring that produces hot air. There is also a mechanical fan that circulates the hot air all over the food at high speed. This hot air cook or fries the food to give the same crispy product as the oil fried variety. The difference between air frying and oil frying is that while oil frying involves immersion of the food into the hot oil to cook, the air fryer doesn't. It means that you can achieve the same cooking results as in oil frying but with little to no oil. There are many heart friendly oils out there, which you can spread over your food before air frying to achieve that fabulous taste. These oils can be used to sprinkle your food before air frying to maintain a healthier diet.

Enjoy your reading!

BREAKFAST RECIPES

Breakfast banana oatmeal

Preparation time: 5 minutes

Cooking time: 12 minutes

Servings: 4

Ingredients:

- 1 cup old-fashioned oats
- 1 cup of coconut milk
- 1 cup of water
- 1 banana, mashed
- 1/2 teaspoon vanilla extract
- 1/2 teaspoon ground cinnamon
- A pinch of grated nutmeg
- A pinch of sea salt

Directions

1. Thoroughly combine all ingredients in a mixing bowl. Spoon the mixture into lightly greased mugs.
2. Then, place the mugs in the air fryer cooking basket.
3. Bake your oatmeal at 380° f for about 12 minutes.

Nutrition: Calories 217; Fat 7g; Carbs 34g; Protein 8g

Classic baked oatmeal

Preparation time: 5 minutes

Cooking time: 10 minutes

Servings: 4

Ingredients:

- 1 cup old-fashioned oats
- 1/4 cup agave syrup
- 1 cup milk
- 1 egg, whisked
- 1 cup apple, chopped
- 1/2 teaspoon baking powder
- 1/2 teaspoon ground cinnamon
- A pinch of grated nutmeg
- A pinch of salt

Directions:

1. Thoroughly combine all ingredients in a mixing bowl. Spoon the mixture into four lightly greased ramekins.

2. Then, place the ramekins in the air fryer cooking basket.

3. Bake your oatmeal at 380° f for about 12 minutes.

4. Enjoy!

Nutrition: Calories 277; Fat 6g; Carbs 45g; Protein 9g; Sugars 20g; Fiber 4g

Old-fashioned granola

Preparation time: 5 minutes

Cooking time: 15 minutes

Servings: 6

Ingredients:

- 1/2 cup rolled oats
- 1/4 cup wheat germ, toasted
- 1/2 cup dried cranberries
- 1/4 cup pumpkin seeds
- 1/4 cup sunflower seeds
- 1/4 cup pecans, chopped
- 1/4 cup walnuts, chopped
- 1/2 teaspoon vanilla extract
- 1/4 cup agave syrup
- 4 tablespoons coconut oil
- 1 teaspoon pumpkin pie

Directions

1. Start by preheating your air fryer to 350° f.
2. Thoroughly combine all ingredients in a lightly greased baking pan.
3. Then, place the pan in the air fryer cooking basket. Bake your granola for about 15 minutes, stirring every 5 minutes.
4. Stock in a closed container for up to three weeks.

Nutrition: Calories 332; Fat 19g; Carbs 38g; Protein 7g

Mushroom and rice bake

Preparation time: 5 minutes

Cooking time: 10 minutes

Servings: 4

Ingredients:

- 1pound brown mushrooms, chopped
- 1 small onion, peeled and chopped
- 2 tablespoons butter, room temperature
- 2 garlic cloves, minced
- Ground black pepper
- Sea salt, to taste
- 1 cup vegetable broth
- 1 ½ cups brown rice, cooked

Directions:

1. Put your air fryer to 360° f.

2. Thoroughly combine all ingredients in a lightly greased baking pan.

3. Lower the pan into the air fryer cooking basket.

4. Cook for about 10 minutes or until cooked through.

Nutrition: Calories 192; Fat 28g; Carbs 6g; Protein 3g

Dried berry bread pudding

Preparation time: 15 minutes

Cooking time: 20 minutes

Servings: 6

Ingredients:

- 2 cups sweet raisin bread, cubed
- 2 eggs, whisked
- 1 cup milk
- 1/2 teaspoon vanilla extract
- 1/4 cup agave syrup
- 1/4 cup dried cherries
- 1/4 cup dried cranberries

Directions:

1. Place the bread cubes in a lightly greased baking pan.
2. In a mixing bowl, thoroughly combine the remaining ingredients.
3. Pour the egg/milk mixture over the bread cubes; set aside for 15 minutes to soak.

20

4. Bake your bread pudding at 350° f for about 20 minutes or until the custard is set but still a little unsteady.

5. Serve at room temperature.

Nutrition: Calories 152; Fat 3g; Carbs 21g; Protein 3g; Sugars 15g

BRUNCH RECIPES

Sausage egg cups

Preparation time: 10 minutes

Cooking time: 10 minutes

Servings: 2

Ingredients:

- 1/4 cup eggbeaters
- 1/4 sausage, cooked and crumbled
- 4 tsp jack cheese, shredded
- 1/4 tsp garlic powder
- 1/4 tsp onion powder
- 4 tbsp spinach, chopped
- Pepper
- Salt

Directions:

1. Mix well all ingredients in a large bowl.
2. Pour batter into the silicone muffin molds and place in the air fryer basket.
3. Cook at 330° f for 10 minutes.
4. Serve and enjoy.

Nutrition: Calories 90; Fat 5g; Carbs 1g; Sugar 2g; Protein 7 g

LUNCH RECIPES

Kipper and balmy orange gravy

Preparation Time: 5 minutes

Cooking Time: 15 minutes,

Servings: 4

Ingredients:

- Cubed, deboned kipper fish, 4
- 2 lemons, sliced
- Balmy vinegar, ¼ cup
- Sweet orange juice, ¼ cup
- A pinch of salt and black pepper

Directions:

1. Barring the fish, mix all the ingredient in a pan
2. Set your air fryer to about 360°F
3. Cook for 5 minutes
4. Insert the kipper
5. Flip lightly and cook in the air fryer 360°F for 10 minutes.
6. Share into dishes and serve immediately alongside a side salad.

Nutrition: Calories 227, fat 9, fiber 12, carbs 14, protein 11

Kipper and pansies

Preparation time: 30 minutes,

Servings: 4

Ingredients:

- Chopped purple onions, 2
- Olive oil, 2 kitchen spoons
- Trimmed and sliced pansies, 2
- Toasted and slice kernels, ¼ cup
- Salt and black pepper to taste
- Deboned kipper fish, 4
- Grilled pansies seeds, 5 teaspoons

Directions:

1. Apply salt and pepper seasoning to the fish
2. Rub 1 kitchen spoon of the oil over it
3. Set your air fryer to 350°F
4. Insert the fish and cook for 5-6 minutes
5. Flip and cook for about 5-6 minutes more
6. Share into dishes
7. Heat 1 kitchen spoon of oil in a pan at about 360°F
8. Insert the onions, swirl, and fry for 2 minutes.
9. Put in pansies seeds and bulbs, kernels, salt, and pepper
10. 1cook for 2-3 minutes more.
11. 1apply the mixture over the fish and dish immediately; enjoy!

Nutrition: Calories 284, fat 7, fiber 10, carbs 17, protein 16

Kipper strips and pinecone mix

Preparation Time: 15 minutes

Cooking Time: 15 minutes

Servings: 2

Ingredients:

- Canned pinecone portions, 8 ounces
- Shredded ginger, a ½ teaspoon
- Olive oil, a little sprinkle
- Pulverized garlic cloves, 2 teaspoons
- Balmy vinegar, i kitchen spoon
- Deboned kipper fish, medium-sized, 2 pieces
- Salt and black pepper to taste

Directions:

1. Rub oil in a pan place the fish in it
2. Insert all the other ingredients
3. Set your air fryer to 350°F
4. Insert the fish and cook for 10 minutes
5. Share into dishes and serve

Nutrition: Calories 236, fat 4, carbs 23, protein 6

Easy kipper strips and bell peppers

Preparation Time: 5 minutes

Cooking Time: 15 minutes

Servings: 6

Ingredients:

- Rough green olives, 1 cup
- Cayenne peppers, 3 pieces divided into average portions
- Smoke-dried pimento, a ½ teaspoon
- Salt and black pepper to taste
- Olive oil, 3 kitchen spoons
- Deboned and skinned kipper fish, 6 average pieces
- Diced coriander, 2 kitchen spoons

Directions:

1. Mix all the ingredients in a pan
2. Set your air fryer to 360°F
3. Insert the mixture and cook for 15 minutes.
4. Share the fish into dishes and serve.

Nutrition: Calories 281, fat 8, fiber 14, carbs 17, protein 16

Kipper and citrus dressing

Preparation Time: 5 minutes

Cooking Time: 10 minutes

Servings: 2

Ingredients:

- Deboned kipper fish, 2
- Orange peel, from ½ of the peel
- Citrus juice, from ½ an orange
- A pinch of salt and black pepper
- Mustard, 2 kitchen spoons
- Honey, 2 teaspoons
- Olive oil, 2 kitchen spoons
- Diced dill, 1 kitchen spoon
- Diced parsley, 2 kitchen spoons

Directions:

1. Place the citrus peel with the citrus juice, salt, pepper, mustard, honey, oil, dill, and parsley
2. Mix and whisk well
3. Insert the kipper into this mixture, and flip
4. Set your air fryer to 350°F
5. Insert the kipper and cook for 5 minutes
6. Flip, and cook for a further 5 minutes
7. Share the fish into dishes, sprinkle the citrus dressing on top, and serve.

Nutrition: Calories 272, fat 8, fiber 12, carbs 15, protein 16

Redfish paella

Preparation Time: 15 minutes

Cooking Time: 30 minutes

Servings: 4

Ingredients:

- Brown rice, 5 ounces
- Garden green beans, 2 ounces
- Chopped and deseeded cayenne pepper
- Chardonnay, 6 ounces
- Chicken broth, 3½ ounces
- Cubed redfish, 1 pound
- Oysters, 6
- Deveined and peeled prawn, 8
- Salt and black pepper to taste
- Olive oil, a little sprinkle

Directions:

1. Put all the ingredients in a pan and flip
2. Set your air fryer to 380°F
3. Insert the mixture and cook for 12 minutes
4. Stir, cook for a further 12 minutes
5. Share into dishes and serve

Nutrition: Calories 290, fat 12, fiber 2, carbs 16, protein 19

Kipper and capers

Preparation Time: 5 minutes

Cooking Time: 12 minutes

Servings: 4

Ingredients:

- Deboned kipper fish, 4 pieces
- Sapped capers, 1 kitchen spoon
- Diced dill, 1 kitchen spoon
- Salt and black pepper to taste
- Lemon juice, from 1 lemon
- Olive oil, 2 teaspoons

Directions:

1. Make a mixture of the capers, dill, salt, pepper, and the oil
2. Coat the fish with the resulting mixture
3. Set your air fryer to 360°F
4. Insert the fish and cook for 6 minutes
5. Flip, cook for a further 6 minutes
6. Share the fish into dishes, sprinkle the lemon juice atop, and serve

Nutrition: Calories 280, fat 11, fiber 1, carbs 12, protein 18

Kipper and jasmine rice

Preparation Time: 10 minutes

Cooking Time: 30 minutes

Servings: 2

Ingredients:

- Deboned wild kipper strips, 2
- Salt and black pepper to taste
- Jasmine rice, ½ cup
- Chicken broth, 1 cup
- Thawed margarine, 1 kitchen spoon
- Saffron, a ¼ teaspoon

Directions:

1. Barring the fish, place all ingredients in a pan
2. Flip and mix well
3. Set your air fryer 360°F
4. Insert the ingredients and cook for 15 minutes.
5. Insert the fish, place on the lid
6. Cook 12 minutes more at the same temperature
7. Share into dishes and serve immediately

Nutrition: Calories 271, fat 8, fiber 9, carbs 15, protein 8

Kipper and carrots

Preparation Time: 5 minutes

Cooking Time: 20 minutes

Servings: 2

Ingredients:

- Deboned kipper strips, 2
- Diced garlic cloves, 3
- Olive oil, 1 kitchen spoon
- Veggie broth, ¼ cup
- Baby carrots, 1 cup
- Salt and black pepper to taste

Directions:

1. Mix the ingredients in a pan
2. Set your air fryer to 370°F
3. Insert the mixture and cook for 20 minutes
4. Share into dishes and serve

Nutrition: Calories 200, fat 6, fiber 6, carbs 18, protein 11

Black cod & plum sauce

Preparation Time: 10 minutes

Cooking Time: 25 minutes

Servings: 2

Ingredients:

- 2 medium black cod fillets; skinless and boneless
- 1 red plum; pitted and chopped
- 2 tsp. Raw honey
- 1/4 tsp. Black peppercorns; crushed
- 1 egg white
- 1/2 cup red quinoa; already cooked
- 2 tsp. Whole wheat flour
- 4 tsp. Lemon juice
- 1/2 tsp. Smoked paprika
- 1 tsp. Olive oil
- 2 tsp. Parsley
- 1/4 cup water

Directions:

1. In a bowl; mix 1 tsp. Lemon juice with egg white, flour and 1/4 tsp. Paprika and whisk well.
2. Put quinoa in a bowl and mix it with ⅓ of egg white mix.
3. Put the fish into the bowl with the remaining egg white mix and toss to coat.
4. Dip fish in quinoa mix; coat well and leave aside for 10 minutes.

5. Heat up a pan with 1 tsp. Oil over medium heat; add peppercorns, honey and plum; stir, bring to a simmer and cook for 1 minute.

6. Add the rest of the lemon juice, the rest of the paprika and the water; stir well and simmer for 5 minutes.

7. Add parsley; stir, take sauce off heat and leave aside for now.

8. Put fish in your air fryer and cook at 380 °F, for 10 minutes. Arrange fish on plates, drizzle plum sauce on top and serve.

Nutrition: calories: 324; fat: 14; fiber: 22; carbs: 27; protein: 22

Fried branzino

Preparation Time: 10 minutes

Cooking Time: 10 minutes

Servings: 4

Ingredients:

- 4 medium branzino fillets; boneless
- 1/2 cup parsley; chopped
- 2 tbsp. Olive oil
- A pinch of red pepper flakes; crushed
- Zest from 1 lemon; grated
- Zest from 1 orange; grated
- Juice from 1/2 lemon
- Juice from 1/2 orange
- Salt and black pepper to the taste

Directions:

1. In large bowl; mix fish fillets with lemon zest, orange zest, lemon juice, orange juice, salt, pepper, oil and pepper flakes
2. Toss really well, transfer fillets to your preheated air fryer at 350° F and bake for 10 minutes; flipping fillets once.
3. Divide fish on plates, sprinkle with parsley and serve right away.

Nutrition: calories: 261; fat: 8; fiber: 12; carbs: 21; protein: 12

French style cod

Preparation Time: 10 minutes

Cooking Time: 22 minutes

Servings: 4

Ingredients:

- White wine, ½ c.
- De-boned cod, 2 lbs.
- Olive oil, 2 tbsps.
- Stewed canned tomatoes, 14 oz.
- Chopped yellow onion,
- Butter, 2 tbsps.
- Black pepper.
- Minced garlic cloves,
- Chopped parsley, 3 tbsps. .
- Salt.

Directions:

1. Set a pan with oil on fire to heat over medium heat.
2. Stir in onion and garlic to cook for 5 minutes.
3. Stir in wine to cook for 1 more minute.
4. Mix in tomatoes to boil for 2 minutes then stir in parsley and remove from heat.
5. Transfer the mix into a heat proof dish that fits the air fryer.

6. Add fish and season it with salt and pepper then cook for 14 minutes at 350°F.
7. Set the fish and tomatoes mix on plates and serve.

Nutrition: Calories: 231, fat: 8, fiber: 12, carbs: 26, protein: 14

Cubed salmon chili

Preparation Time: 10 minutes

Cooking Time: 10 minutes

Servings: 12

Ingredients:

- Olive oil, 2 tbsps.
- Black pepper.
- Chopped red chilies,
- Flour, 1/3 c.
- Egg,
- Water, ¼ c.
- Balsamic vinegar, ¼ c.
- Minced garlic cloves,
- Shredded coconut, 1¼ c.
- Honey, ½ c.
- Cubed salmon, 1 lb.
- Salt.

Directions:

1. Combine salt and flour in a mixing bowl.
2. Have another mixing bowl in place to combine black pepper and egg.
3. In a third bowl, put the coconut.
4. Pass the salmon cubes through flour, egg then coconut and place them into the air fryer.
5. Allow to cook for 8 minutes at 370°F and shake halfway.
6. Set the salmon cubes on plates.

7. Set a pan with water on fire to boil over medium high heat.

8. Stir in honey, vinegar, chilies and cloves to boil under low heat.

9. Drizzle the mix on salmon to serve.

10. Enjoy.

Nutrition: Calories: 220, fat: 12, fiber: 2, carbs: 14, protein: 13

Creamy tuna cakes

Preparation time: 15 minutes

Cooking time: 15 minutes

Servings: 4

Ingredients:

- 2: 6-ouncescans tuna, drained
- 1½ tablespoon almond flour
- 1½ tablespoons mayonnaise
- 1 tablespoon fresh lemon juice
- 1 teaspoon dried dill
- 1 teaspoon garlic powder
- ½ teaspoon onion powder
- Pinch of salt and ground black pepper

Directions:

1. Preheat the air fryer to 400°F and grease an air fryer basket.
2. Mix the tuna, mayonnaise, almond flour, lemon juice, dill, and spices in a large bowl.
3. Make 4 equal-sized patties from the mixture and arrange in the air fryer basket.
4. Cook for about 10 minutes and flip the sides.
5. Cook for 5 more minutes and dish out the tuna cakes in serving plates to serve warm.

Nutrition: Calories: 200, fat: 11g, carbohydrates: 9g, sugar: 8g, protein: 24g, sodium: 122mg

DINNER RECIPES

Cheeseburger-stuffed bell peppers

Preparation time: 15 minutes

Cooking time: 20 minutes

Servings 4 / 360°F

Ingredients

- Olive oil
- 4 large red bell peppers
- 1-pound lean ground beef
- 1 cup diced onion
- Salt
- Freshly ground black pepper
- 1 cup cooked brown rice
- ½ cup shredded reduced-fat cheddar cheese
- ½ cup tomato sauce
- 2 tablespoons dill pickle relish
- 2 tablespoons ketchup
- 1 tablespoon Worcestershire sauce
- 1 tablespoon mustard
- ½ cup shredded lettuce
- ½ cup diced tomatoes

Instructions

1. Spray a fryer basket lightly with olive oil.
2. Cut about ½ inch off the tops of the peppers. Remove any seeds from the insides. Set aside.

3. In a large skillet over medium-high heat, cook the ground beef and onion until browned, about 5 minutes. Season with salt and pepper.

4. In a large bowl, mix together the ground beef mixture, rice, cheddar cheese, tomato sauce, relish, ketchup, Worcestershire sauce, and mustard.

5. Spoon the meat and rice mixture equally into the peppers.

6. Place the stuffed peppers into the fryer basket. Air fry until golden brown on top, 10 to 15 minutes.

7. Top each pepper with the shredded lettuce and diced tomatoes and serve.

Nutrition: Calories: 366; total fat: 11g; saturated fat: 5g; cholesterol: 75mg; carbohydrates: 33g; protein: 32g; fiber: 6g; sodium: 612mg

Steak and veggie kebabs

Preparation Time: 2 Hours

Cooking Time: 15 Minutes

Servings 4

Ingredients

- ½ cup soy sauce
- 3 tablespoons lemon juice
- 2 tablespoons Worcestershire sauce
- 2 tablespoons Dijon mustard
- 1 teaspoon minced garlic
- ¾ teaspoon freshly ground black pepper
- 1-pound sirloin steak, cut into 1-inch cubes
- 1 medium red bell pepper, cut into big chunks
- 1 medium green bell pepper, cut into big chunks
- 1 medium red onion, cut into big chunks
- Olive oil

Directions

1. In a small bowl, whisk together the soy sauce, lemon juice, Worcestershire sauce, Dijon mustard, garlic, and black pepper. Divide the marinade equally between two large zip-top plastic bags.
2. Place the steak in one of the bags, seal, and refrigerate for at least 2 hours. Place the vegetables in the other bag, seal, and refrigerate for 1 hour.
3. If using wooden skewers, soak the skewers in water for at least 30 minutes.
4. Spray a fryer basket lightly with olive oil.

48

5. Thread the steak and veggies alternately onto the skewers.

6. Place the skewers in the fryer basket in a single layer. You may need to cook the skewers in batches.

7. Air fry for 8 minutes. Flip the skewers over, lightly spray with olive oil, and cook until the steak reaches your desired level of doneness, an additional 4 to 7 minutes. The internal temperature should read 125°F for rare, 135°F for medium rare, 145°F for medium and 150°F for medium well.

Nutrition: Calories: 271; total fat: 7g; saturated fat: 3g; cholesterol: 65mg; carbohydrates: 12g; protein: 38g; fiber: 2g; sodium: 2,147mg

Korean BBQ beef bowls

Preparation Time: 2 Hours

Cooking Time: 25 Minutes

Servings 4

Ingredients

- ½ cup soy sauce
- 2 tablespoons brown sugar
- 2 tablespoons red wine vinegar or rice vinegar
- 1 tablespoon olive oil, plus more for spraying
- 1 tablespoon sesame oil
- 1-pound flank steak, sliced very thin against the grain
- 2 teaspoons cornstarch
- 2 cups cooked brown rice
- 2 cups steamed broccoli florets

Directions

1. In a large bowl, whisk together the soy sauce, brown sugar, vinegar, olive oil, and sesame oil. Add the steak, cover with plastic wrap, and refrigerate for at least 30 minutes or up to 2 hours.
2. Spray a fryer basket lightly with olive oil.
3. Remove as much marinade as possible from the steak. Reserve any leftover marinade.
4. Place the steak in the fryer basket in a single layer. You may need to cook the steak in batches.
5. Air fry for 10 minutes. Flip the steak over and cook until the steak reaches your desired level of doneness, an additional 7 to 10 minutes.

The internal temperature should read 125°f for rare, 135°f for medium rare, 145°f for medium, and 150°f for medium well. Transfer the steak to a large bowl and set aside.

6. While the steak is cooking, in a small saucepan over medium-high heat, bring the remaining marinade to a boil.

7. In a small bowl, combine the cornstarch and 1 tablespoon of water to create a slurry. Add the slurry to the marinade, lower the heat to medium-low, and simmer, stirring, until the sauce starts to thicken, a few seconds to 1 minute.

8. Pour the sauce over the steak and stir to combine.

9. To assemble the bowls, spoon ½ cup brown rice and ½ cup of broccoli into each of four bowls and top with the steak.

Nutrition: Calories: 399; total fat: 15g; saturated fat: 1g; cholesterol: 45mg; carbohydrates: 36g; protein: 29g; fiber: 3g; sodium: 1,875mg

SIDE DISH RECIPES

Batter-fried scallions

Preparation time: 5 minutes

Cooking time: 5 minutes

Servings: 4

Ingredients:

- Trimmed scallion bunches,
- White wine, 1 cup
- Salt, 1 tsp.
- Flour, 1 cup
- Black pepper, 1 tsp.

Directions:

1. Set the air fryer to heat up to 3900f. Using a bowl, add and mix the white wine, flour and stir until it gets smooth. Add the salt, the black pepper and mix again. Dip each scallion into the flour mixture until it is properly covered and remove any excess batter. Grease your air fryer basket with nonstick cooking spray and add the scallions. At this point, you may need to work in batches.

2. Leave the scallions to cook for 5 minutes or until it has a golden-brown color and crispy texture, while still shaking it after every 2 minutes. Carefully remove it from your air fryer and check if it's properly done. Then allow it to cool before serving. Serve and enjoy.

Nutrition: Calories: 190 fat: 22g protein: 4g carbs: 9g

Heirloom tomato with baked feta

Preparation time: 20 minutes

Cooking time: 14 minutes

Servings: 4

Ingredients:

- 8 oz. Feta cheese
- Salt
- 2 heirloom tomatoes
- ½ cup sliced red onions
- 1 tbsp. Olive oil
- For the basil pesto
- ½ cup grated parmesan cheese
- Salt
- ½ cup olive oil
- 3 tbsps. Toasted pine nuts
- ½ cup chopped basil
- 1 garlic clove
- ½ cup chopped parsley

Directions:

1. Prepare the pesto.
2. Put the toasted pine nuts, garlic, salt, basil, and parmesan in a food processor. Process until combined.
3. Gradually add oil as you mix. Process until everything is blended.
4. Transfer to a bowl and cover. Refrigerate until ready to use.

5. Slice the feta and tomato into round slices with half an inch thickness. Use paper towels to pat them dry.

6. Spread a tbsp. Of pesto on top of each tomato slice.

7. Top with a slice of feta.

8. In a small bowl, mix a tbsp. Of olive oil and red onions.

9. Scoop the mixture on top of the feta layer. Arrange them in the cooking basket. Cook for 14 minutes at 390° F.

10. Transfer to a platter and add a tbsp. Of basil pesto on top of each. Sprinkle them with a bit of salt before serving.

Nutrition: calories: 493 fat: 423g carbs: 61g protein: 169g

CASSEROLES

Creamy cheesy tomato casserole

Preparation time: 5 minutes

Cooking time: 30 minutes

Servings: 4

Ingredients:

- 5 eggs
- 2 tablespoons heavy cream
- 3 tablespoons chunky tomato sauce
- 2 tablespoons grated parmesan cheese

Directions:

1. Prepare a mixing bowl, then add the eggs and cream.
2. Mix in the tomato sauce and add the cheese.
3. Spread into a glass baking dish and cook at 350 °F for 30 minutes.
4. Top with extra cheese and serve.

Nutrition: Calories: 50 Fat: 5g Carbs: 3g Protein: 4g

CHICKEN AND POULTRY

Classic smoked pork chops

Preparation time: 10 minutes

Cooking time: 20 minutes

Servings: 6

Ingredients:

- 6 pork chops
- Hickory smoked salt, to savor
- Ground black pepper, to savor
- 1 teaspoon onion powder
- 1/2 teaspoon garlic powder
- 1/2 teaspoon cayenne pepper
- 1/3 cup almond meal

Directions

1. Gently put all ingredients into a zip top plastic bag; shake them up to coat well.
2. Spritz the chops with a pan spray (canola spray) works well here and transfer them to the air fryer cooking basket.
3. Roast them for 20 minutes at 375 °f. Serve with sautéed vegetables.

Nutrition: 332 calories 17g fat 8g carbs 48g protein

Pork ribs with red wine sauce

Preparation time: 3 hours

Cooking time: 25 minutes

Servings: 4

Ingredients:

- For the pork ribs:
- 1 ½ pounds pork ribs
- 2 tablespoons olive oil
- 1/2 teaspoon freshly cracked black peppercorns
- 1/2 teaspoon hickory smoked salt
- 1 tablespoon Dijon mustard
- 2 tablespoons coconut aminos
- 2 tablespoons lime juice
- 1 clove garlic, minced
- For the red wine sauce:
- 1 ½ cups beef stock

- 1 cup red wine
- 1 teaspoon balsamic vinegar
- 1/4 teaspoon salt

Directions:

1. Place all ingredients for the pork ribs in a large sized mixing dish. Cover and marinate in your refrigerator overnight or at least 3 hours.
2. Air fry the pork ribs for 10 minutes at 320° f.
3. Meanwhile, make the sauce. Add a beef stock to a deep pan preheated over a moderate flame; boil until it is reduced by half.
4. Add the remaining ingredients and increase the temperature to high heat. Let it cook for further 10 minutes or until your sauce is reduced by half.
5. Serve the pork ribs with red wine sauce. Bon appétit!

Nutrition: Calories 438 Fat 23g Carbs 3g Protein 32g

Pork with buttery broccoli

Preparation time: 15 minutes

Cooking time: 30 minutes

Servings: 4

Ingredients:

- 1 ½ pounds blade steaks skinless, boneless
- Kosher salt
- Ground black pepper, to taste
- 2 garlic cloves, crushed
- 2 tablespoons coconut aminos
- 1 tablespoon oyster sauce
- 2 tablespoon lemon juice
- 1pound broccoli, broken into florets
- 2 tablespoons butter, melted
- 1 teaspoon dried dill weed
- 2 tablespoons sunflower seeds, lightly toasted

Directions:

1. Start by preheating your air fryer to 385° f. Spritz the bottom and sides of the cooking basket with cooking spray.

2. Now, season the pork with salt and black pepper. Add the garlic, coconut aminos, oyster sauce, and lemon juice.

3. Cook for 20 minutes then turn over halfway through the cooking time.

4. Toss the broccoli with the melted butter and dill. Add the broccoli to the cooking basket and cook at 400° f for 6 minutes, shaking the basket periodically.

5. Serve the warm pork with broccoli and garnish with sunflower seeds.

Nutrition: Calories 346 Fat 11g Carbs 4g Protein 32g

Pork sausage with mashed cauliflower

Preparation time: 10 minutes

Cooking time: 30 minutes

Servings: 6

Ingredients:

- 1pound cauliflower, chopped
- 1/2 teaspoon tarragon
- 1/3 cup Colby cheese
- 1/2 teaspoon ground black pepper
- 1/2 onion, peeled and sliced
- 1 teaspoon cumin powder
- 1/2 teaspoon sea salt
- 3 beaten eggs
- 6 pork sausages, chopped

Directions

1. Boil the cauliflower until tender. Then, purée the cauliflower in your blender.
2. Transfer to a mixing dish along with the other ingredients.

3. Divide the prepared mixture among six lightly greased ramekins; now, place ramekins in your air fryer.
4. Bake in the preheated air fryer for 27 minutes at 365° f. Eat warm.

Nutrition: Calories 506 Fat 42g Carbs 6g Protein 28g

BEEF, STEAK AND LAMB RECIPES

Rosemary beef chuck roast

Preparation time: 10 minutes

Cooking time: 45 minutes

Servings: 6

Ingredients:

- 1 (2poundbeef chuck roast
- 1 tablespoon olive oil
- 2 teaspoons dried rosemary, crushed
- Salt, as required

Directions:

1. .in a bowl, add the oil, herbs and salt and mix well.
2. Coat the beef roast with herb mixture generously.
3. Arrange the beef roast onto the greased enamel roasting pan.
4. Select air fry of air fryer oven and adjust the temperature to 360 ° f.
5. Set 45 minutes and press "start/stop" to begin preheating.

6. When the unit beeps to show that it is preheated, insert the roasting pan in the oven.

7. Get the pan from the oven and place the roast onto a cutting board.

8. With a piece of foil, cover the beef roast for about 20 minutes before slicing.

9. With a sharp knife, cut the beef roast into desired size slices and serve.

Nutrition: Calories: 358 Fat: 19g Carbs: 6g Protein: 34g

Beef round roast with carrots

Preparation time: 15 minutes

Cooking time: 8 hours

Servings: 6

Ingredients:

- 1 (2poundbeef round roast
- 3 large carrots, peeled and chopped
- 1 large yellow onion, sliced thinly
- 1 cup tomato sauce
- 1 teaspoon ground cumin
- ½ teaspoon ground cinnamon
- Salt and ground black pepper, as required

Directions:

1. In an oven safe pan that will fit in the air fryer oven, place all ingredients and stir to combine.
2. Cover the pan with a lid.
3. Arrange the pan over the wire rack.
4. Select slow cooker of air fryer oven and set on "low".

5. Set the timer for 8 hours and press "start/stop" to begin cooking.

6. Take the pan from the oven and place the roast onto a cutting board for about 10-15 minutes before slicing.

7. Cut into desired sized slices and serve.

Nutrition: Calories: 269 Fat: 11g Carbs: 18g Protein: 21g

FISH AND SEAFOODS

Cod fillets and peas

Preparation time: 10 minutes

Cooking time: 10 minutes

Servings: 4

Ingredients:

- 4 cod fillets, boneless
- 2 tablespoons parsley, chopped
- 2 cups peas
- 4 tablespoons wine
- ½ teaspoon oregano, dried
- ½ teaspoon sweet paprika
- 2 garlic cloves, minced
- Salt and pepper to the taste

Directions:

1. In your food processor mix garlic with parsley, salt, pepper, oregano, paprika, and wine, blend well.
2. Rub fish with half of this mix, place in your air fryer and cook at 360 ° f for 10 minutes.
3. Meanwhile, put peas in a pot, add water to cover, add salt, bring to a boil over medium high heat.
4. Cook for 10 minutes, drain and divide among plates.
5. Also divide fish on plates, spread the rest of the herb dressing all over and serve.
6. Enjoy!

Nutrition: calories 261, fat 8, fiber 12, carbs 20, protein 22

Coconut coated fish cakes with mango sauce

Preparation: 20 minutes

Cooking time: 14 minutes

Servings: 4

Ingredients:

- 18 ounces of white fish fillet
- 1 green onion, finely chopped
- 1 mango, peeled, cubed
- 4 tablespoons of ground coconut
- 1½ ounces of parsley, finely chopped
- 1½ teaspoons of ground fresh red chili
- 1 lime, juice and zest
- 1 egg
- 1 teaspoon of salt

Directions:

1. Add ½ ounce of parsley, ½ teaspoon of ground chili, half of the lime juice and zest to the mango cubes and mix thoroughly.
2. Using a food processor, puree the fish and add the salt, egg, and lime zest, lime juice and chili. Stir in the green onions, 2 tablespoons of coconut and the rest of the parsley.

3. Put the rest of the coconut in a shallow dish. Mold the fish mixture into 12 round cakes. Place the cakes in the coconut to coat them.

4. Put half of the cakes into the fryer basket and bake for 7 minutes at 356°f. Remove when cakes are golden and bake the second batch of cakes.

5. Serve the cakes with the mango salsa.

Nutrition: Calories: 200 Fat: 13g Carbs: 8g Protein: 14g

Teriyaki glazed halibut steak

Preparation: 30 minutes

cooking time: 1015 minutes

servings: 3

Ingredients

- 1-pound halibut steak for the marinade:
- 2/3 cup low sodium soy sauce
- ½ cup mirin
- 2 tablespoons lime juice
- ¼ cup sugar
- ¼ cup orange juice
- ¼ teaspoon ginger ground
- ¼ teaspoon crushed red pepper flakes
- 1 each garlic clove (smashed)

Directions

1. Place all the ingredients for the teriyaki glaze/marinade in a saucepan. Bring to a boil and lessen by half, then let it cool.
2. When it cools, pour half of the glaze/marinade into a Ziploc bag together with the halibut then refrigerate for 30 minutes.
3. Preheat the air fryer to 390°f. Place the marinated halibut into the air fryer and cook 10-12 minutes. Brush some of the glaze that's left over the halibut steak.
4. Spread over white rice with basil/mint chutney.

Nutrition: Calories: 280 Fat: 7g Carbs: 14g Protein: 37g

FRUIT AND
VEGETABLES

Platter of brussels and pine nuts

Preparation time: 10 minutes

Cooking time: 35 minutes

Serving: 6

Ingredients

- 15 ounces of brussels sprouts
- 1 tablespoon of olive oil
- 1 and a 3/4 ounce of drained raisins
- Juice of 1 orange
- 1 and a 3/4-ounce toasted pine nuts

Directions:

1. Take a pot of boiling water and add sprouts, boil for 4 minutes
2. Transfer them to cold water and drain them, store them in a freezer and allow them to cool
3. Take raising and soak them in orange juice for 20 minutes
4. Preheat your fryer to 392 degrees Fahrenheit
5. Take a pan and pour oil and stir fry your sprouts
6. Transfer the sprouts to the cooking basket and roast for 15 minutes
7. Serve the sprouts with a garnish of raisins, pine nuts, orange juice
8. Enjoy!

Nutrition: Calories: 267 Fat: 25g Dietary fiber: 6g Protein: 7g

SNACK RECIPES

Banana fritters

Preparation Time: 10 minutes

Cooking Time: 15 minutes

Servings: 8

Ingredients:

- 8 bananas
- 3 tablespoons vegetable oil
- 3 tablespoons corn flour
- 1 egg white
- ¾ cup breadcrumbs

Directions:

1. Preheat the air fryer to 350° f. And combine the oil and breadcrumbs, in a small bowl. Coat the bananas with the corn flour first, brush them with egg white, and dip them in the breadcrumb mixture.
2. Arrange on a lined baking sheet and cook for 8 minutes.

Nutrition: Calories: 203 Protein: 4 grams Fat: 3 grams Carbohydrates: 35 grams

Tasty banana snack

Preparation Time: 10 minutes

Cooking Time: 15 minutes

Servings: 8

Ingredients:

- 16 baking cups crust
- 1 banana; peeled and sliced into 16 pieces
- ¼ cup peanut butter
- A ¾ cup of chocolate chips
- 1 tablespoon vegetable oil

Directions:

1. Put chocolate chips in a small pot, heat up over low heat; stir until it melts and takes off heat.
2. In a bowl; mix peanut butter with coconut oil and whisk well.
3. Spoon 1 teaspoon chocolates mix in a cup, add 1 banana slice and top with 1 teaspoon butter mix.
4. Repeat with rest of the cups, place them all into a dish that fits your air fryer, cook at 320° f. For 5 minutes; transfer to a freezer and keep there until you serve them as a snack.

Nutrition: Calories: 70 Protein: 1-gram Fat: 4 grams Carbohydrates: 10 grams

Strawberry cobbler

Preparation Time: 10 minutes

Cooking Time: 25 minutes

Servings: 6

Ingredients:

- A ¾ cup of sugar
- 6 cups strawberries, halved
- 1/8 teaspoon baking powder
- 1 tablespoon lemon juice
- ½ cup flour
- A pinch of baking soda
- A ½ cup of water
- 3 and ½ tablespoon olive oil
- Cooking spray

Directions:

1. In a bowl, mix strawberries with half of the sugar, sprinkle some flour, add lemon juice, whisk and pour into the baking dish that fits your air fryer and greased with cooking spray.
2. In another bowl, mix flour with the rest of the sugar, baking powder and soda and stir well.

3. Add the olive oil and mix until the whole thing with your hands.

4. Add ½ cup water and spread over strawberries.

5. Introduce in the fryer at 355° f. And bake for 25 minutes.

6. Leave cobbler aside to cool down, slice and serve.

7. Enjoy!

Nutrition: Calories: 221 Protein: 9 grams Fat: 3 grams Carbohydrates: 6 grams

Super yummy brownies

Preparation Time: 10 minutes

Cooking Time: 25 minutes

Servings: 4

Ingredients:

- 4ounces of softened unsalted butter
- 8ounces of bittersweet chocolate chips
- 3 eggs
- 1 cup of granulated sugar
- ½ teaspoon of salt
- 1 cup of all-purpose flour

Directions:

1. Preheat your air fryer to 350° F.
2. Grease a heat safe dish that is convenient with your air fryer.
3. Using a saucepan, soften the butter and chocolate.
4. Then using a large bowl, add and mix all the ingredients properly.
5. Add the brownie batter to the greased heat safe dish and smoothen the surface.
6. Place it in your air fryer and cook it for 25 minutes or until a toothpick comes out clean in the center.
7. Remove the brownies and allow it to chill it is cool enough to eat, thereafter cut it into squares. Serve and enjoy!

Nutrition: Calories: 130 Protein: 2 grams Fat: 5 grams Carbohydrates: 21 grams

Grilled scallion cheese sandwich

Preparation Time: 10 minutes

Cooking Time: 20 minutes

Servings: 1

Ingredients:

- 2 teaspoons butter (room temperature
- ¾ cup grated cheddar cheese
- 2 slices of bread
- 1 tablespoon grated parmesan cheese
- 2 scallions (thinly sliced

Directions:

1. Spread a teaspoon of butter on a slice of bread. Place it in the cooking basket with the buttered side facing down.
2. Add scallions and cheddar cheese on top. Spread the rest of the butter in the other slice of bread. Place it on top of the sandwich and sprinkle with parmesan cheese.
3. Cook for 10 minutes at 356° f.
4. Serve and enjoy!

Nutrition: Calories: 511 Protein: 26 grams Fat: 34 grams Carbohydrates: 19 grams

APPETIZER RECIPES

Maple carrot fries

Preparation time: 10 minutes

Cooking time: 12 minutes

Servings: 6

Ingredients:

- 1 lb. Carrot, peeled and cut into sticks
- 1 teaspoon maple syrup
- 1 teaspoon olive oil
- ½ teaspoon ground cinnamon
- Salt, to taste

Directions:

1. In a bowl, add all the ingredients and mix well.
2. Press "power button" of air fry oven and turn the dial to select the "air fry" mode.
3. Press the time button and again turn the dial to set the cooking time to 12 minutes
4. Now push the temp button and rotate the dial to set the temperature at 400° f.
5. Press "start/pause" button to start.
6. When the unit beeps to show that it is preheated, open the lid.
7. Arrange the carrot fries in "air fry basket" and insert in the oven.
8. Serve warm.

Nutrition: calories 41 total fat 8 g saturated fat 1 g cholesterol 0 mg sodium 79 mg carbs 3 g fiber 2 g sugar 4 g protein 6 g

PASTA AND RICE
RECIPES

Spanish Rice

Preparation Time: 5 minutes

Cooking Time: 14 minutes

Servings 4 to 6

Ingredients:

- 2 tablespoons butter
- 2 cups long grain rice
- 8 ounces (227 g) tomato sauce
- 1½ cups chicken stock or water
- 1 teaspoon chili powder
- 1 teaspoon cumin
- ½ teaspoon onion powder
- ½ teaspoon garlic powder
- ½ teaspoon salt

Directions:

1. Set your Instant Pot to Sauté and melt the butter.
2. Add the rice and sauté for about 4 minutes, stirring occasionally.
3. Add the remaining ingredients to the Instant Pot and stir.
4. Secure the lid and set the cooking time for 10 minutes at High Pressure.
5. When the timer beeps, perform a natural pressure release for 10 minutes, then release any remaining pressure. Carefully remove the lid.
6. Use spatula or fork to fluff the rice. Serve warm.

Nutrition: Calories: 141 Fat: 8g Carbs: 13g Protein: 2g

BREAD & GRAINS

Sunflower seeds bread

Preparation time: 15 minutes

Cooking time: 18 minutes

Servings: 4

Ingredients:

- 2/3 cup whole-wheat flour
- 2/3 cup plain flour
- 1/3 cup sunflower seeds
- ½ sachet instant yeast
- 1 teaspoon salt
- 2/3-1 cup lukewarm water

Directions:

1. In a bowl, mix the flours, sunflower seeds, yeast, and salt.
2. Slowly, add in the water, stirring continuously until a soft dough ball form.
3. Now, move the dough onto a lightly floured surface and knead for about 5 minutes using your hands.
4. Make a ball from the dough and place into a bowl.
5. With a plastic wrap, cover the bowl and place at a warm place for about 30 minutes.
6. Set the temperature of air fryer to 390°f. Grease a cake pan. (6"x 3")
7. Coat the top of dough with water and place into the prepared cake pan.
8. Arrange the cake pan into an air fryer basket.
9. Air fry for about 18 minutes or until a toothpick inserted in the center comes out clean.

10. Remove from air fryer and place the pan onto a wire rack for about 10-15 minutes.

11. Carefully, take out the bread from pan and put onto a wire rack until it is completely cool before slicing.

12. Cut the bread into desired size slices and serve.

Nutrition: Calories: 177 Carbohydrate: 33 g Protein 5 g Fat 4 g Sugar 2 g

DESSERT RECIPES

Mixed berry crumble

Preparation time: 10 minutes

cooking time: 11 to 16 minutes

servings: 4

Ingredients

- ½ cup chopped fresh strawberries
- ½ cup fresh blueberries
- ⅓ cup frozen raspberries
- 1 tablespoon freshly squeezed lemon juice
- 1 tablespoon honey
- ⅔ cup whole-wheat pastry flour (see tip
- 3 tablespoons packed brown sugar
- 2 tablespoons unsalted butter, melted

Directions

1. In a 6 by 2 inch pan, combine the strawberries, blue-berries, and raspberries. Drizzle with the lemon juice and honey.
2. In a small bowl, mix the pastry flour and brown sugar.
3. Stir in the butter and mix until crumbly. Sprinkle this mixture over the fruit.
4. Bake for 11 to 16 minutes, or until the fruit is tender and bubbly and the topping is golden brown. Serve warm.

Nutrition calories: 199; fat: 6g (27% of calories from fat; saturated fat: 4g; protein: 3g; carbohydrates: 35g; sodium: 1mg; fiber: 4g;

Apple blueberry hand pies

Preparation time: 20 minutes

cooking time: 7 to 9 minutes

servings: 4

Ingredients

- 1 medium granny smith apple, peeled and finely chopped
- ½ cup dried blueberries
- 1 tablespoon freshly squeezed orange juice
- 1 tablespoon packed brown sugar
- 2 teaspoons cornstarch
- 4 sheets frozen phyllo dough, thawed
- 8 teaspoons unsalted butter, melted
- 8 teaspoons sugar
- Nonstick cooking spray, for coating the phyllo dough

Directions

1. In a medium bowl, mix the apple, blueberries, orange juice, brown sugar, and cornstarch.
2. Place 1 sheet of phyllo dough on a work surface with the narrow side facing you. Brush very lightly with 1 -teaspoon of butter and sprinkle with 1 teaspoon of sugar. Fold the phyllo sheet in half from left to right.
3. Place one fourth of the fruit filling at the bottom of the sheet in the center. Fold the left side of the sheet over the filling. Spray lightly with cooking spray.
4. Fold the right side of the sheet over the filling. Brush with 1 teaspoon of butter and sprinkle with 1 teaspoon of sugar.

5. Fold the bottom right corner of the dough up to meet the left side of the pastry sheet to form a triangle. Continue folding the triangles over to enclose the filling, as you would fold a flag. Seal the edge with a bit of water.

6. Spray lightly with cooking spray. Repeat with the remaining 3 sheets of the phyllo, butter, sugar, and cooking spray, making four pies.

7. Place the pies in the air fryer basket. Bake for 7 to 9 -minutes, or until golden brown and crisp. Remove the pies and let cool on a wire rack before serving.

Nutrition calories: 239; fat: 8g (30% calories from fat; saturated fat: 5g; protein 2g; carbohydrates: 42g; sodium: 34mg; fiber: 5g;

Oatmeal carrot cookie cups

Preparation time: 10 minutes

cooking time: 8 to 10 minutes

servings: 16 cups

Ingredients

- 3 tablespoons unsalted butter, at room temperature
- ¼ cup packed brown sugar
- 1 tablespoon honey
- 1 egg white
- ½ teaspoon vanilla extract
- ⅓ cup finely grated carrot (see tip
- ½ cup quick cooking oatmeal
- ⅓ cup whole-wheat pastry flour
- ½ teaspoon baking soda
- ¼ cup dried cherries

Directions

1. In a medium bowl, beat the butter, brown sugar, and honey until well combined.
2. Add the egg white, vanilla, and carrot. Beat to combine.
3. Stir in the oatmeal, pastry flour, and baking soda.
4. Stir in the dried cherries.

5.   Double up 32 mini muffin foil cups to make 16 cups. Fill each with about 4 teaspoons of dough. Bake the cookie cups, 8 at a time, for 8 to 10 minutes, or until light golden brown and just set. Serve warm.

Nutrition calories: 127; fat: 5g (35% calories from fat; saturated fat: 3g; protein: 2g; carbohydrates: 20g; sodium: 88mg; fiber: 1g;

Dark chocolate oatmeal cookies

Preparation time: 10 minutes

cooking time: 8 to 13 minutes

servings: 30 cookies

Ingredients

- 3 tablespoons unsalted butter
- 2 ounces dark chocolate, chopped (see tip
- ½ cup packed brown sugar
- 2 egg whites
- 1 teaspoon pure vanilla extract
- 1 cup quick cooking oatmeal
- ½ cup whole-wheat pastry flour
- ½ teaspoon baking soda
- ¼ cup dried cranberries

Directions

1. In a medium metal bowl, mix the butter and dark -chocolate. Bake in the air fryer for 1 to 3 minutes, or until the butter and chocolate melt. Stir until smooth.
2. Beat in the brown sugar, egg whites, and vanilla until smooth.
3. Stir in the oatmeal, pastry flour, and baking soda.

4. Stir in the cranberries. Form the dough into about 30 (1inchballs. Bake the dough balls, in batches of 8, in the air fryer basket for 7 to 10 minutes, or until set.

5. Carefully remove the cookies from the air fryer and cool on a wire rack. Repeat with the remaining dough balls.

Nutrition calories: 55; fat: 2g (33% of calories from fat; saturated fat: 1g; protein: 1g; carbohydrates: 8g; sodium: 25mg; fiber: 1g;

Tasty banana and cinnamon cake

Preparation Time: 10 minutes

Cooking Time: 30 minutes

Servings: 4

Ingredients:

- Butter, soft 1 tbsp.
- Egg 1
- Brown sugar ⅓ cup.
- Honey 2 tbsp.
- Banana; peeled and mashed 1
- White flour 1 cup.
- Baking powder 1 tsp.
- Cinnamon powder ½ tsp.
- Cooking spray

Directions :

1. Take a cake pan and spritz some cooking spray on it. Leave the pan aside.
2. Add butter with sugar, banana, honey, egg, cinnamon, baking powder, flour in a bowl and whisk all the ingredients together.
3. Now, take the greased cake pan and pour this batter into the pan.
4. Set your air fryer at 350° f for 30 minutes and introduce the pan into the fryer to cook for the given time.
5. Let the cake cool down in room temperature.
6. Cut cakes into slices, serve and enjoy this delicious cake.

Nutrition: Calories 232, fat 4, fiber 1, carbs 34, protein 4

Delicious banana bread

Preparation Time: 15 minutes

Cooking Time: 40 minutes

Servings: 6

Ingredients:

- Sugar ¾ cup.
- Butter 1/3 cup.
- Vanilla extract 1 tsp.
- Egg 1
- Bananas ; mashed 2
- Baking powder 1 tsp.
- Flour 1 and ½ cups.
- Baking soda ½ tsps.
- Milk 1/3 cup.
- Cream of tartar 1 and ½ tsps.
- Cooking spray

Directions:

1. Take a bowl and mix milk with cream of tartar, sugar, butter, egg, vanilla, bananas and stir everything together.
2. Gather another bowl to add flour with baking powder and baking soda.
3. Blend these two mixtures together and grease a cake pan with the cooking spray.

4. Pour the batter into the greased cake pan and place it into the air fryer to cook at 320°f for 40 minutes.

5. Take the bread out of the fryer and let it cool down in room temperature.

6. Slice the bread evenly and enjoy by serving it immediately.

Nutrition: Calories 292, fat 7, fiber 8, carbs 28, protein 4

Easy to make air fried bananas

Preparation Time: 10 minutes

Cooking Time: 10 minutes

Servings: 4

Ingredients:

- Butter 3 tbsp.
- Eggs 2
- Bananas ; peeled and halved 8
- Corn flour ½ cup.
- Cinnamon sugar 3 tbsp .
- Panko 1 cup.

Directions:

1. Take a pan to melt the butter over medium high heat.
2. Add panko into the pan and give it a stir.
3. Let it cook for 4 minutes and then transfer to a bowl.
4. Coat the bananas with flour, egg, panko mix and arrange them properly in your air fryer basket.
5. Sprinkle some cinnamon sugar on top and set the fryer at 280°f for 10 minutes to cook.
6. Once cooked, serve immediately.

Nutrition: Calories 164, fat 1, fiber 4, carbs 32, protein 4

Dark Chocolate Truffles

Preparation Time: 15 minutes

Cooking Time: 15 minutes

Servings: 10

Ingredients:

- cups dark chocolate chips, melted
- ¼ cup coconut oil
- tbsp. orange juice
- 1 tsp vanilla extract
- ½ cup honey
- 1 tbsp. heavy cream
- tbsp. flour
- ¼ cup cocoa powder

Directions:

1   Preheat fryer to 240° F.
2   Combine all ingredients except cocoa powder until smooth. Mixture will be thick.
3   Shape into balls and roll to the cocoa powder.
4   Bake for 10 minutes.
5   Cool, serve, and enjoy!

Nutrition: Calories: 180 Fat: 12g Carbs: 16g Protein: 2g

Rum Cake

Preparation Time: 15 minutes

Cooking Time: 35 minutes

Servings: 8

Ingredients:

- 1 cup walnuts, chopped
- 1 package yellow cake mix
- 1 package vanilla pudding mix
- large eggs
- ½ cup water
- ½ cup vegetable oil
- ½ cup dark rum

Directions:

1 Turn on the air fryer to 330 ° F. Spray a cake pan that will fit into the air fryer with non-stick spray.

2 Combine all ingredients and mix well. Pour into prepared cake pan.

3 Bake for 30 minutes.

4 Cool completely before serving.

5 Enjoy!

Nutrition: Calories: 225 Fat: 12g Carbs: 24g Protein: 3g

CONCLUSION

Thank you for reading all this book!

Anyone can make the recipes out of the air fryer. You need to know the right measurements, and you will have a great recipe ready for you. Once you know how to cook with an air fryer, you would want to cook in it every time. There are various recipes found in this book to try, so get started now without wasting any time!

You have already taken a step towards your improvement.

Best wishes!